SURVIVE YOUR DIVORCE

AND LEARN TO LIVE JOYFULLY AGAIN

Nakia M. Evans

ALL RIGHTS RESERVED. No part of this report may be modified or altered in any form whatsoever, electronic, or mechanical, including photocopying, recording, or by any informational storage or retrieval system without express written, dated and signed permission from the author.

AFFILIATE DISCLAIMER. The short, direct, non-legal version is this: Some of the links in this report may be affiliate links which means that I earn money if you choose to buy from that vendor at some point in the near future. I do not choose which products and services to promote based upon which pay me the most, I choose based upon my decision of which I would recommend to a dear friend. You will never pay more for an item by clicking through my affiliate link, and, in fact, may pay less since I negotiate special offers for my readers that are not available elsewhere.

DISCLAIMER AND/OR LEGAL NOTICES: The information presented herein represents the view of the author as of the date of publication. Because of the rate with which conditions change, the author reserves the right to alter and update his opinion based on the new conditions. The report is for informational purposes only. While every attempt has been made to verify the information provided in this report, neither the author nor his affiliates/partners assume any responsibility for errors, inaccuracies or omissions. Any slights of people or organizations are unintentional. If advice concerning legal or related matters is needed, the services of a fully qualified professional should be sought. This report is not intended for use as a source of legal or accounting advice. You should be aware of any laws which govern business transactions or other business practices in your country and state. Any reference to any person or business whether living or dead is purely coincidental.

Copyright ©2023 Nakia M. Evans

TABLE OF CONTENTS

INTRODUCTION

CHAPTER 1: SURVIVING A DIVORCE

How to Survive the Workday During a Divorce

CHAPTER 2: FINANCES DURING A DIVORCE

CHAPTER 3: KIDS AND DIVORCE

CHAPTER 4: AFTER THE DIVORCE

Getting the Most From Your Divorce

CHAPTER 5: FINDING JOY AGAIN

Happiness
Fun

CHAPTER 6: CONCLUSION

BONUS: DIVORCE CHECKLISTS

"DIVORCE ISN'T JUST THE PERSON, IT'S EVERYTHING THAT GOES WITH IT – YOUR KIDS, THE ADJUSTMENT, EVERYTHING."

- ALANA STEWART

INTRODUCTION

Divorce is classified by psychologists as one of the most stressful experiences anyone can face. A divorce radically changes a family if children are involved. There can be great financial pressure. Your self-esteem can take a hit. You might feel embarrassed. You might have a lot of doubt and fear regarding the future.

It's a lot to manage and overcome.

You might believe that you'll never be happy again. **While this might feel real at the moment, it's up to you how the rest of your life progresses.** It's a pretty safe bet that your divorce and the aftermath won't be as bad as you anticipate.

In fact, a divorce can be a ***new beginning*** for a life that's more fulfilling and filled with joy. It won't happen overnight, but you might be on the cusp of a more meaningful and enjoyable existence.

Consider these topics as a means to survive your divorce and create a new, happy life:

Chapter 1:
Surviving a Divorce.
The first step is surviving, and then you can worry about the rest. While getting through a divorce is certainly challenging, nearly one million people do it each year in the US. You can, too, with these tips.

Chapter 2:
Finances During a Divorce.
Finances are always important, but a divorce magnifies their relevance. Many people facing a divorce make financial errors during this critical time. Avoid being one of them.

Chapter 3:
Kids and Divorce.
Everyone worries about the children in a divorce. Children struggle but are quite resilient. Talking with them the right way sets them up for a positive outcome.

Chapter 4:
After the Divorce.
It's time to celebrate this considerable victory but the work is only beginning. Now you have a wonderful opportunity in front of you. Make the most of it.

Chapter 5:
Finding Joy Again.
It might not feel like joy is possible, but it is. Happiness with a little fun sprinkled on top is all you need to have a joyful life.

Chapter 6:
Conclusion.
You're just at the beginning of the rest of your life. How will you spend it?

"WHAT WE WAIT AROUND A LIFETIME FOR WITH ONE PERSON, WE CAN FIND IN A MOMENT WITH SOMEONE ELSE."

— STEPHANIE KLEIN, STRAIGHT UP AND DIRTY

CHAPTER 1:
SURVIVING A DIVORCE

The first step to moving on with your life is surviving the divorce process itself. If you've made the decision to get divorced, you're likely feeling a combination of relief and fear. If your partner made the decision, you might be feeling betrayed or unwanted.

These feelings can be overwhelming, but they do eventually pass. Keeping this fact in mind will make the process easier. Just knowing that there is a light at the end of the tunnel can keep you sane.

While all divorces are unique, there are certain people that manage the divorce process more successfully than others.

These personality traits can help you survive divorce:

1. Optimism.
One thing that greatly benefits anyone going through a divorce is a positive attitude about the future. Divorce is incredibly stressful. The belief that everything will turn out okay in the end is very powerful.

● Optimism can make all the difference in the world. Imagine the difference in your day-to day life between believing that the rest of your life is doomed versus everything will be okay. You might even believe that this is the best thing that could have happened long-term.

● Force yourself to examine the positive possibilities in every situation. For example, you might be annoyed that you had to park at the back of the parking lot. What is good about this? Exercise, for one. Or, maybe it's the chance to spend a few more minutes outside in the sun.

2. Resilience.

Divorce is filled with ups and downs. Some days are much worse than others. Some days are better, too! Resilience is always a positive trait to possess, but it can be especially helpful during divorce.

● The ability to weather any situation that occurs during and after the divorce process is golden.

● Resilience is affected by optimism and the ability to relax. If you're pessimistic or stressing yourself out, your resilience will falter.

3. Creativity.

You'll experience a variety of new challenges during and after divorce. New problems require new solutions. Those that are able to think creatively have an advantage.

● Brainstorm solutions to your challenges. Spend some time each day generating ideas.

4. Cool under pressure.

This one is a given. You're likely to experience more stress than you've ever had to deal with before. Dealing with stress effectively can enhance your career, relationships, and general outlook on life.

● Look into ways that lower the amount of stress you feel in your life. Meditation, progressive relaxation, and visualization are three of many tools available.

5. Delegate.

Meeting with your attorney, packing, looking for a place to live, moving, and all the other things that can go along with divorce take time, time you probably don't have to spare.

● You're also likely to need financial advice. You might need help mowing the grass or cleaning the house. Perhaps you'll need the assistance of a mental health professional.

● After the divorce, you may need help with all the things your spouse used to do for your family.

● With all these new demands, you're going to need all the help you can get. Some people like to take care of everything themselves, but the ability to delegate can ease the divorce process.

6. Organized.

If there was ever a time that would tax your multitasking skills, a divorce proceeding is that time. Between meetings, paperwork, deadlines, and appointments, it's enough to challenge even the most organized person

- If you're naturally disorganized, this is one of the most popular topics in any bookstore. There's no shortage of information on this issue.
- As a side note, one of the greatest predictors of success is conscientiousness. Conscientious people are organized.

How many of these traits do you have?

All of these traits are skills that you can learn. The personality you've developed to this point in your life might not be ideal for dealing effectively with a divorce, but you can make a few adjustments and smooth your journey.

Interestingly, these traits are also effective for many other parts of your life. They can help your career and your relationships.

Practicing these skills will help, but other tips will help, too.

Consider these general tips for surviving a divorce:

1. Take a deep breath and hold on.
You already know it's going to be a bumpy ride, but it might not be nearly as challenging as you anticipate. On the other hand, it might be worse. It's impossible to predict how your spouse is going to handle this situation.

● Remind yourself there are almost a million divorces in the US each year. **Your odds of physical and emotional survival are staggeringly high.** It's important to try to relax as much as possible, handle your business, and persevere.

2. Maintain your social connections.
Men have this issue more often than women. Some people choose to withdraw when stressed. *This is a huge mistake.*

● Isolating yourself will magnify your negative feelings and leave you feeling lonely and alone. **You need your friends and family more than ever.** Lean on them.

3. Have fun.
Divorce isn't fun, but there's no law that says you can't enjoy yourself. Continue to get out of the house. Spend time with your friends and do the things you enjoy. **Life doesn't have to stop just because you're getting divorced.**

● Go to a coffee shop. Your favorite coffee shop can provide a comfortable and productive familiarity. A coffee shop is a great place to go to get out of isolation and be around people without being directly interrupted. New coffee shops are popping up in neighborhoods day by day. I've been in a few good ones lately for meetings.

4. Visualize a positive future.
If you want to make yourself miserable, expect to have a horrible future. On the other hand, imagining a positive future that appeals to you will help you to feel happier.

5. Maintain your grooming.
One of the major signs that someone's mental health is going off the rails is a significant decrease in grooming standards.
- It's easy to convince yourself that you really don't need a haircut, your hair & nails done, or "Who needs makeup?" you may ask yourself. However, this is a slippery slope.
- Maintain your grooming routine. It will help you to feel more normal and grounded. Once your grooming slides, other things begin to slide, too.

6. Maintain your sleep schedule.
Do your best to stay on track with your sleep. It can be easy to worry yourself late into the night or to spend a Saturday in bed. However, neither is a good idea.

Relax as much as you can and hold on tight. Maintain your friendships and continue to take care of yourself. It's easy to withdraw and neglect yourself. Your physical and mental health will suffer as a result.

"IT'S NOT THE LOAD THAT BREAKS YOU DOWN, IT'S THE WAY YOU CARRY IT."
LENA HORNE

How to Survive the Workday During a Divorce

Most of us don't have the luxury of just sitting at home during a divorce. We still have to make a living. In fact, making a living might be more important than ever. Work can provide a sanctuary of sorts. You can get your mind off your relationship woes. But it can also be a challenge. It's not always easy to focus when your personal life is in turmoil. You also have to deal with the inevitable questions that always come with a divorce.

Surviving your workday is part of surviving divorce.

Use these strategies:

1. Consider how much and with whom you're going to share your divorce news. Do you just want to get the information out there or would you prefer to keep your head down? Both options have advantages and disadvantages. Take some time to think about it.

2. Only do work at work.
It can be tempting to use your spare time to read emails from your lawyer or go over divorce-related paperwork, but this can make things worse. You'll not only be distracted from your regular work, but you may also be putting your job in jeopardy. *This would be a horrible time to lose a job.*

● Work can be a nice break from the challenges you face in your social life. Avoid ruining that potential oasis by taking care of divorce-related matters at home.

3. Tell your boss.
Assuming your relationship with your boss is at least cordial, let them know what's going on. You're sure to get a little slack and some consideration when there's extra work to be doled out.

● Your boss will appreciate the heads up and be more accommodating if you need time off or need to leave early.

4. Inform human resources.
You may need to make adjustments to your insurance and other benefits. Your human resources department has been through this situation many times before and they can help you with all the necessary paperwork.

5. Have your story prepared.
Even if you try to keep your divorce a secret, it won't stay that way. You'll eventually receive questions, sympathy, or offers for support in one form or another. How will you handle this?

● Have a story ready. Some people will want to know what happened. Others will offer to help you with your kids or to perform errands. Some will share their own experiences or offer advice.

6. Be mindful. This just means to keep your mind on your work. At work, you're not meeting with your attorney, being questioned by a judge, or arguing with your soon-to-be ex-spouse. Since your reality at the moment is work, keep your focus on your work.

- Once your attention wanders to your divorce, it will be hard to stop that train. The day will be much more enjoyable if you can keep your mind on work.

While a few people at your place of work are just nosey, most of them will have a genuine concern for you. Don't be afraid to accept a few offers for assistance. Sometimes you'll need a babysitter, a listening ear, or a shoulder to cry on.

It's a mistake to refuse the help that's offered to you. You would be happy to help someone else, so allow others to help you. Remember that your job is probably pretty important to your life. Bills don't go away just because you're getting divorced. Do the best job you can at work but be sure to let your boss know about your situation.

"WHEN YOU RISE IN THE MORNING, GIVE THANKS FOR THE LIGHT, FOR YOUR LIFE, FOR YOUR STRENGTH. GIVE THANKS FOR YOUR FOOD AND FOR THE JOY OF LIVING. IF YOU SEE NO REASON TO GIVE THANKS, THE FAULT LIES IN YOURSELF."
- TECUMSEH

CHAPTER 2:
FINANCES DURING A DIVORCE

Divorce is stressful. Financial challenges are stressful. Combining the two is enough to keep anyone up at night! Financial issues can be quite complicated. It's difficult to give a lot of blanket advice since divorce laws vary so much from state to state.

Your attorney will be your best source of information regarding your finances during the divorce. Ensure you get advice from a qualified source and use it. Your cubicle mate and your parents are not qualified sources.

Take your finances seriously during your divorce with these smart strategies:

1. Only take advice from experts.
Your Aunt Sallie may be the wisest woman you know, and maybe she went through a divorce in the 70's, but Aunt Nora is the last place you should be asking for divorce-related financial advice.

- Divorce attorneys have professional education and years of experience doing little more than dealing with divorces.

- It doesn't make sense to get advice from non-experts. Take care of yourself by getting the best help you can.

2. Understand your budget.

It's important to understand your expenses for the present and the future. In many relationships, one spouse handles all of the financial matters.

- You might not have the slightest idea what it costs to live at your current standard of living. You might be in for a present surprise or quite a shock. This information can be useful for future planning.

3. Avoid major financial decisions.

Not only will a judge raise eyebrows at buying a new boat or cleaning out your bank account and gifting the money to your mother, but it's also just not a good time to take on large financial obligations.

- *Your ability to make sound decisions is compromised when you're stressed. Proceed carefully.*

4. It's time to be thrifty.

Divorce attorneys aren't cheap. Setting up a new life isn't cheap either. Consider some of the expenses of setting up a new life:

- Moving expenses
- Deposit/down payment and rent/mortgage
- Utility deposits
- Utility bills - water, gas, phone, cable, internet
- Furniture
- Food
- Automobile-related expenses
- Furniture

These are just the highlights. *Downsize and save money now. You may need it later.*

5. Keep track of your credit report. This is especially important if you have any joint debts or credit cards. Your spouse might suddenly decide that paying the mortgage on the house isn't a priority anymore. This would damage your credit.
● Sometimes, one spouse will decide to max out the credit card figuring that their soon-to be ex will have to pay half the bill.
● It's important to stay on top of these issues.

6. Open an individual bank account and credit card.
Get these in place as soon as possible. The credit card can be used for any expenses and to build your credit. These items might be more challenging to accomplish after your divorce is finalized.

Your attorney is likely to have a lot of additional advice. Be sure to follow it to the letter. Money issues can be stressful, so give this topic the attention it deserves. It will be much easier to move on with your life if your financial house is in order.

"WHEN TWO PEOPLE DECIDE TO GET A DIVORCE, IT ISN'T A SIGN THAT THEY 'DON'T UNDERSTAND' ONE ANOTHER, BUT A SIGN THAT THEY HAVE, AT LAST, BEGUN TO."
- HELEN ROWLAND

CHAPTER 3:
KIDS AND DIVORCE

It's always challenging to explain divorce to children. How you handle this important issue will largely depend on the age of the children. Explaining the situation to an 8-year-old is different than explaining it to a 15-year-old. You'll need to adjust your approach depending on the child's characteristics.

Of course, it will be a difficult time for any child. However, there are many things you can do to ease the transition for the little ones in your life.

Use these techniques to make the best of a bad situation with your children:

1. Resist the urge to address the issue with your children without your spouse present. While the relationship with your spouse might be adversarial, it will be beneficial for your children if you present a united front.

Get together and talk to your children about the changes that are coming.

2. Choose a good time to talk. Right before your child's baseball game wouldn't be an ideal time. Choose a time when there is nothing going on afterward. Everyone will need some quiet time to process news like this.

3. Anticipate questions. Teenage children are likely to have questions about staying at the same school. Younger children will be worried about their living arrangements. *Try to anticipate the questions your children will ask and work out the answers with your spouse beforehand.*

4. Ensure that the children know that the divorce has nothing to do with them. Children often feel guilty in divorce situations. Ensure they understand that sometimes adults decide they don't want to stay together. This has nothing to do with the behavior of the children.

5. Be ready for tears. Actually, be ready for any reaction from sadness, to anger, to feigned indifference. Continue to reassure them.

6. Contact their teacher. Let your child's teacher know about the situation. A younger child is likely to have some issues at school. Let their teacher know what's going on. A little extra compassion might be needed when dealing with any issues at school.

7. Explain the plan going forward. Present a general outline of what their lives will look like in the days and months ahead. **Let them know what will stay the same and what will change.**

8. Be extra kind to your spouse. It will help your children a lot if you and your spouse are especially nice to each other going forward. Let the kids see that they're not going to be in the middle of a war for the rest of their lives. It will be good for your relationship with your future ex, too.

Children can be particularly affected by divorce, but also possess an amazing resiliency. Your children will greatly benefit if you and your spouse can remain civil before, during, and after the divorce process. Be open with your children and tolerant of unusual behavior. I waited until my kids were 28 & 30 to get divorced and it was still hard on the family.

> *"THE JOY OF LIFE COMES FROM OUR ENCOUNTERS WITH NEW EXPERIENCES, AND HENCE THERE IS NO GREATER JOY THAN TO HAVE AN ENDLESSLY CHANGING HORIZON, FOR EACH DAY TO HAVE A NEW AND DIFFERENT SUN."*
> - CHRISTOPHER MCCANDLESS

CHAPTER 4:
AFTER THE DIVORCE

The divorce is over, but the work isn't done quite yet. Now it's time to rebuild your life. This is a great opportunity to make changes and improvements. Everything is up in the air at this point, **so make the most the possibilities.** You can begin building the life you've always dreamed of. It won't be easy, but it will be so worth it!

General tips for dealing with life after divorce:

1. Celebrate. You did it! You survived what was probably the most challenging situation of your life. You can expect the majority of your life to be easy, relatively speaking, by comparison.

● Any challenge you successfully navigate will make you a stronger and more resilient person. Surviving a divorce can give you the confidence to conquer other obstacles.

2. Stay in touch with your current friends. It's natural that you may lose some friends. After all, some of your pre-divorce friends were closer to your spouse than they were to you.

- This doesn't mean that you have to lose all of your friends. Maintain as many of your good relationships as you can.
- Divorce requires starting over in many ways, but that doesn't mean you have to start over from absolute ground zero.

3. **Make a few positive changes.** It can be easier to make some positive changes since you have all this momentum on your side and a new life. Many people find divorce is a great time to:
- Join a gym
- Buy new clothes
- Get a new haircut
- Learn a new language
- Learn yoga
- Start an online business
- Think about new habits you can add to your life
- Consider old habits you might want to eliminate

4. **Drop some dead weight.** You're on a roll now. With all this change going on, take full advantage of it. *It's the perfect time to cut out undesirable activities and people from your life.*
- We all accumulate people and activities that drain our spirit, patience, or bank account without a reasonable return on our investment. Where possible, let these things and people go

5. **Join a community.** You might consider yourself an introvert, but you have a need to be part of a community. There are many types of communities you can join:
- Religious/spiritual
- Sports team

● Various clubs - men's clubs, women's clubs, motorcycle clubs, and so on.
● Find a group of people with whom you have similar interests and participate. You'll feel better and more secure.

6. Forgive your ex. You might be totally justified in the hatred you feel toward your ex when you think about their icy heart, but they don't care. You're only making yourself miserable.
● In reality, your ex did as well as they could. Maybe their best just wasn't good enough.
● Forgiving your ex will set you free.

7. Forgive yourself.
No one is without blame in a divorce. You probably believe that you made your share of mistakes, too. But everyone makes mistakes. The best you can do is to learn from your mistakes and forgive yourself. Getting divorced is the first step on your new journey. Now it's important to survive the aftermath and create a life you can enjoy going forward.

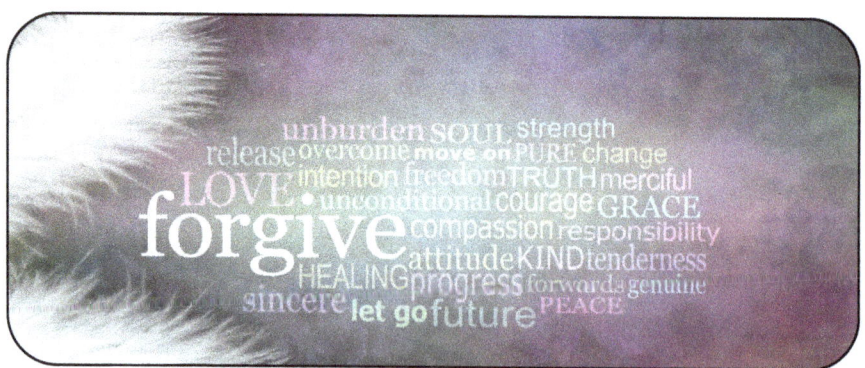

"Living in the moment means letting go of the past and not waiting for the future. It means living your life consciously, aware that each moment you breathe is a gift."
- OPRAH WINFREY

Getting the Most From Your Divorce

The best part of a divorce is the opportunity to start over. Be sure to take full advantage of this great chance to create a new life. What do you want to do with it? You can do better than just surviving your divorce. You can even thrive afterward. Difficult times are often ripe with opportunities. **Decide that you're going to get everything you can out of this experience.** There are benefits to a divorce. It's up to you to take advantage of them.

Use these tips to make the most of your challenging situation:

1. Learn from it.
You can learn a lot from a divorce. For example, you can make positive adjustments to your approach to dating and marriage.
- What did you like or dislike about your spouse?
- What mistakes did you make in your relationship?
- What characteristics do you need in a partner?
- What characteristics can you simply not tolerate?

Learn everything you can from your previous relationship and figure out ways to use that information to your advantage in the future. You're starting your life over in many ways. Take what you've learned and put it to good use.

2. Make new friends. You have some extra space in your life now. Fill it with a few new friends. You're able to have a wider variety of friends when you're single. Take advantage of the opportunity to add to your social circle.

3. Seek out your old, lost friends. We lose a few friends over time. We may get too busy, or life circumstances make it difficult or awkward to maintain certain relationships.

● While it's nice to think that all true friendships are for life, that's rarely the case. Depending on your life and that of the other person, you may not be compatible at certain stages of life.

● Since you've undergone a significant change and may have additional free time on your hands, now might be a great time to reach out to a few friends that you've lost touch with.

● Few things are as comforting as a familiar face. You have a lot of catching up to do!

4. Find new hobbies. There's something that you've always wanted to do or learn but haven't yet. It's finally time! Be open to doing something new. It might boost your social life, too.

5. Embrace self-improvement. This can be anything from losing weight to learning how to be more patient. Think about the person you'd like to be and take a strong step in that direction.

A divorce might be uncomfortable, but it can be a real opportunity, too. There are few times in your life that you have the freedom to change your life so radically

> "WHEN PEOPLE DIVORCE, IT'S ALWAYS SUCH A TRAGEDY. AT THE SAME TIME, IF PEOPLE STAY TOGETHER IT CAN BE EVEN WORSE."
> - MONICA BELLUCCI

CHAPTER 5: FINDING JOY AGAIN

What exactly is joy? It's a combination of fun or pleasure and happiness. It's possible to have fun in the moment, yet not be happy. It's also possible to be happy without having a lot of pleasure or fun.

Joy means you have both in your life.

Happiness

People have been pondering for thousands of years about what it takes to be happy. It's easy to see that different people have differing beliefs on what creates happiness.

- Some people believe that happiness is all about money. Others believe that money is the root of all evil.
- Others focus on success.
- Others believe happiness comes from having a lot of love in your life.
- Some people think that reaching their ultimate potential is the key to happiness.

There's no end to the theories surrounding happiness.

However, **most psychologists believe that the primary drive of a human is comfort and happiness.** People just convince themselves of different paths to reach that goal. Arguably, someone who has chosen a life on Wall Street and someone who has chosen to slog around in a third-world country feeding the poor are really motivated by the same thing - happiness.

What will it take to make you happy?

There are several things that make happiness more likely to occur, such as:

1. Sufficient financial resources.
There's no rule that says you can't be happy and poor, but it does make it more challenging. A smaller income makes it more challenging to pay your bills, buy food and clothes, and enjoy yourself.
● Excessive debt is often mentioned as something that diminishes happiness.
● *Studies show that happiness increases with income to around $75,000. More than that doesn't seem to make people any happier.*

2. Something to look forward to. Remember how excited you were when your birthday or Christmas was on the horizon. Positive anticipation really adds something to our lives.

- This could be a vacation, a date on Saturday, or something you're going to buy for yourself when you attain a goal.

3. Sufficient social circle. How many people do you need in your life? Some need a lot more than others! Most of us need at least a couple of friends to be happy and content.

4. Someone to love and someone to love you. One thing that sets people apart from other creatures is the ability to love and the ability to appreciate love. There are a variety of relationships that can provide this.

5. A purpose. Whether your purpose is to end world hunger, write the world's greatest screenplay, or be the best possible parent, we all need a purpose. It's up to you to figure out that purpose.

6. Self-esteem. If you don't feel good about yourself, how can you be happy? Be a person that you admire. You already know all the things you can't stand about yourself. It's necessary to either change them or accept them.

7. A lack of things that make you miserable. Happiness isn't just a collection of certain attributes and situations, it's the absence of things that detract from happiness

- Consider the low-rated parts of your life and do what is necessary to lift them up.

Happiness is half of joy. Are you allowing happiness to happen in your life? Do you have the basics in place, so happiness can grow and flourish? Also, remember that the negative things in your life can greatly inhibit the amount of happiness you can experience. Be sure to remove those negative things.

There's no guaranteed formula for happiness, but you know what you like and don't like. You also know what you need and don't need. Those are good places to start.

<u>Fun</u>

What is fun? ***Fun is basically an enjoyable distraction from everyday life and stresses.*** It's a pleasant change of pace. It's an opportunity to laugh and connect with others under enjoyable circumstances.

What's the difference between happiness and fun? Happiness is a pervasive feeling that you carry throughout the day. Fun is temporary. ***Those things that are fun will never make you happy, but they are part of experiencing joy.***

Sex, ice cream, and playing basketball is fun, but you can have your fill of them. Twelve hours of sex isn't enjoyable, and neither is eating five gallons of ice cream. You never get tired of happiness, though.

Consider these common myths that can prevent you from having fun:

1. You believe that you can't have fun without spending money. There is plenty of fun to be had for free. Parks, the beach, watching a movie on TV, social networking, and plenty more. The options are only limited by your imagination.

2. You're too serious. Life is a death sentence, and no one gets out alive. Life is short, so enjoy it as much as you can. Life doesn't have to be a solemn experience. You can be serious enough to get the most out of life while still having a great time along the way. Lighten up!

3. You're too picky. Some people require perfection to have a good time. They go to the beach, but they're complaining that it's a little too hot and too crowded, or they see someone 20 yards away they don't like.
- *If the conditions or people in your life have to be perfect for you to enjoy yourself, you're doomed to always be unhappy.*

4. You require too much to have fun. Some of us can have fun playing horseshoes and grilling hot dogs with friends. Others require box seats to watch the Celtics play the Lakers. If you have a healthy value system and a reasonable outlook on life, you can find fun anywhere.

Fun can be had quite easily if you allow it to happen. If you're one of those people that has a lot of requirements, you're missing out on a lot. Look around you and notice all the ways you could be enjoying yourself. Life is short, so avoid taking it too seriously.

> "DIVORCE IS NOT THE END OF THE WORLD. IT'S WORSE TO STAY IN AN UNHEALTHY MARRIAGE. THAT'S A WORSE EXAMPLE FOR THE CHILDREN."
> — JERRY HALL

Add more fun to your life with these activities:

1. Spend time learning something that interests you. It doesn't have to be academic, but it could be. You might be fascinated by scuba diving or shooting a bow and arrow. Learning something new can be a load of fun, as long as you're interested in the topic.

- Avoid being too serious here. This is about having fun, not furthering your career. Learning Mandarin might be great for your career, but if it doesn't interest you, it won't be fun.
- Imagine you were forced to become an expert on something strictly for your own entertainment. What would you choose?

2. Embrace the idea of having fun. This goes back to being too serious. There's a time to take care of business and a time to let loose and have a good time. Fun should be a priority in your life. Be open to the idea of having fun and you'll have more of it.

3. Be spontaneous. Real fun doesn't have to be planned a week in advance. Interesting opportunities for fun present themselves all the time. You might be passing by a pub you've never seen before, stumble on a German festival, or see a large group of people performing yoga in the park. Experience more!

● *Are you open to an invitation to do something fun without any notice?*

4. Make a list of things you enjoy. You don't have to be spontaneous. You can take the bull by the horns and make your own fun. **Remind yourself of all the things you enjoy doing and make plans to do them.**

● If you have a list, you'll never be at a loss for what you can do to have fun.

5. Make a list of things that sound fun to you that you've never done. No one has done everything. There are still plenty of things you probably want to try. Now might be just the time to do them!

Have some fun! When you combine fun with happiness, you're able to experience joy in your life. This might feel like a long journey after a divorce, but you might arrive there quicker than you think! Everyone has the right to experience joy, even you.

CHAPTER 6:
CONCLUSION

Divorce can be incredibly challenging for everyone involved, including children. However, it's possible to live joyfully again. The first step is to survive the divorce. This includes maintaining your social network, dealing with any financial issues, supporting your children, maintaining your productivity at work, and taking care of yourself, mentally & physically.

Expert advice is essential during a divorce. Your friends, family, and co-workers might mean well, but it's important to get help from a professional.

Finding joy again means rebuilding your life. **It's a beautiful opportunity hidden inside a great challenge.** You can really use a divorce to build an incredible life. You'll rarely have such a great opportunity with so many possibilities.

Joy is a combination of happiness and fun. While fun is enjoyable, it can never lead to happiness. Fun is part of a well-balanced life and a critical component of joy. Happiness is unique to each person, but there are general ideas you can put to good use.

Divorce can be a new beginning for everyone involved. Hold on tight and do your best. You can survive divorce and live joyfully again! I survived!

About the author, Nakia Evans

In January 2023, Nakia filed for divorce after her marriage fell apart several year earlier.

Nakia raised 3 children, now ages 28, 28, and 30, and has two grandchildren.

Nakia is a Realtor in Maryland and North Carolina. She enjoys time with her friends & family, traveling, shopping, volunteering in leadership roles, and working in multiple states with real estate agents and entrepreneurs. Multiple income opportunities keep Nakia busy. She enjoys her time on stage speaking to thousands of guests at corporate conferences, hosting events, and coaching via the internet. Most of all Nakia enjoys spending time building new relationships and relocating to NC full-time.

In 2022, Nakia made major decisions related to her future, including starting a new romantic friendship in a new state, where she now resides and works.

Nakia survives divorce with the support of close friends and family members. Nakia's divorce drama was not shared with everyone. That was very important to her because she didn't want to cause distractions or burden friends and family with worry over the past few years.

Nakia coaches real estate leaders an publishes self-help books monthly, offering most at a heavily discounted cost. She is known on social media for providing daily motivation and inspiration to all walks of life.

Connect with Nakia at MovingWithNakia.com

DIVORCE CHECKLIST

ACTIVITIES

- Consider the impact of divorce on your taxes and estate planning.
- Consider hiring a divorce lawyer or mediator.
- Prepare emotionally for the process and seek support from friends and family.
- Think about child custody and visitation arrangements, if applicable.
- Determine your living arrangements during and after the divorce process.
- Consider counseling.
- Gather important documents such as marriage certificate, prenuptial agreement, financial statements, bank statements, tax returns, and property deeds.
- Make a list of joint assets and debts.
- Open a separate bank account and start saving money.

POST DIVORCE TO DO

ACTIVITIES

- Update legal documents (will, power of attorney, etc.)
- Close joint bank accounts and credit cards.
- Change beneficiaries on life insurance policies and retirement accounts.
- Cancel or transfer utility bills and other shared expenses.
- Update your address and contact information.
- Seek counseling or support if needed.
- Create a budget and financial plan for the future.
- Take care of yourself physically and emotionally.
- Consider updating your social media and online profiles.
- Start exploring new hobbies and interests to help you move forward.
- Meet new people and have fun!
- Be sure to update friends and family.

TO-DO LIST

TOP PRIORITIES:
1.
2.
3.
4.
5.
6.
7.

APPOINTMENTS:
1.
2.
3.
4.
5.
6.
7.

BUSINESS TO-DO:
- [ ]
- [ ]
- [ ]
- [ ]
- [ ]
- [ ]
- [ ]
- [ ]
- [ ]
- [ ]
- [ ]
- [ ]
- [ ]
- [ ]

PERSONAL TO-DO:
- [ ]
- [ ]
- [ ]
- [ ]
- [ ]
- [ ]
- [ ]
- [ ]
- [ ]
- [ ]
- [ ]
- [ ]
- [ ]
- [ ]

NOTES:

URGENT BUT NOT A PRIORITY:

TO-DO LIST

TOP PRIORITIES:
1. _____
2. _____
3. _____
4. _____
5. _____
6. _____
7. _____

APPOINTMENTS:
1. _____
2. _____
3. _____
4. _____
5. _____
6. _____
7. _____

BUSINESS TO-DO:
- [ ] _____
- [ ] _____
- [ ] _____
- [ ] _____
- [ ] _____
- [ ] _____
- [ ] _____
- [ ] _____
- [ ] _____
- [ ] _____
- [ ] _____
- [ ] _____
- [ ] _____

PERSONAL TO-DO:
- [ ] _____
- [ ] _____
- [ ] _____
- [ ] _____
- [ ] _____
- [ ] _____
- [ ] _____
- [ ] _____
- [ ] _____
- [ ] _____
- [ ] _____
- [ ] _____
- [ ] _____

NOTES:
_____
_____
_____
_____

URGENT BUT NOT A PRIORITY:
_____
_____
_____
_____

www.ingramcontent.com/pod-product-compliance
Lightning Source LLC
Chambersburg PA
CBHW061516040426
42450CB00008B/1653